ABC's

Of Wonderful Women

Nora Kane

Parson's Porch Books

ABC's Of Wonderful Women

ISBN: Softcover 978-0692437384
Copyright © 2015 by Nora Kane

All rights reserved. No part of this book may be reproduced or transmitted in any form or by any means, electronic or mechanical, including photocopying, recording, or by any information storage and retrieval system, without permission in writing from the publisher.

To order additional copies of this book, contact:

Parson's Porch Books
1-423-475-7308
www.parsonsporch.com

Parson's Porch Books is an imprint of Parson's Porch & Company (PP&C) in Cleveland, Tennessee. PP&C is an innovative non-profit organization which raises money by publishing books of noted authors, representing all genres. All donations from contributors and profits from publishing are shared with the poor.

Aa

A is for Anna Julia Cooper, she loved to teach and sing.
She saw God live in everyone and the good that they can bring

Bb

B is for bravery, that's what Anna Julia Cooper knew. She used her songs to free the slaves by water to wade through.

Cc

C is for courageous, like our friend Sojourner Truth. She pointed to a man and said Jesus wasn't born from you.

"where did your Christ come from? From God and from a woman. Man had nothing to do with Him."

Dd

D is for Dorothy Day, she sided with the poor. She wrote in papers and went to jail to say no to the war.

Ee

E is for endless, like the love these women showed. They loved women and they love the world, with beaming light they glowed.

Ff

F is for Frida Kahlo, who felt much pain and much despair.
But she fought for revolution and she painted from her chair.

Gg

G is for Georgia O'Keefe, she painted many flowers.
She kicked tradition and went out West to show us woman power.

Hh

H is for hearts, beating bold and true. Like all the hearts of all these women who paved the way for you.

Ii

I is for Isadora Duncan, she leaped away from rules. A flowing dance was her religion and she taught it in her school.

زل

J is for justice, like Pauli Murray dreamed of. She fought the odds for her degree and preached her words of love.

K is for keeping on, even when the road seems long.
Frida Kahlo and Maya Angelou remind you to be strong.

L is for love, it was Mother Teresa's way. Through simple works for those least wanted she brought light into the day.

Missionaries of Charity

"the most terrible poverty is lonliness and the feeling of being unloved"

Mm

M is for Mary Daly, who said God is not a man. She did away with old traditions, on male dominance she put a ban.

Nn

N is for no limits, like the visions of these women. Their paintings, poems, and dances show the hard work they have given.

O is for original, like each one of these women. By being true to being you, you enrich the world we live in.

you are a unique and valuable member of this world, and no two stars shine the same.

Pp

P is for playful, because we can't forget the fun. Dance and sing and go adventure like these women would have done.

Qq

Q is for quiet, which may not seem so brave. But when we're quiet we can listen to hear what others say.

listen with your heart so that you may understand

Listening is an act of love.

Rr

R is for resistance, like that of Sojourner Truth. She changed religion for black women and her sermons are the proof.

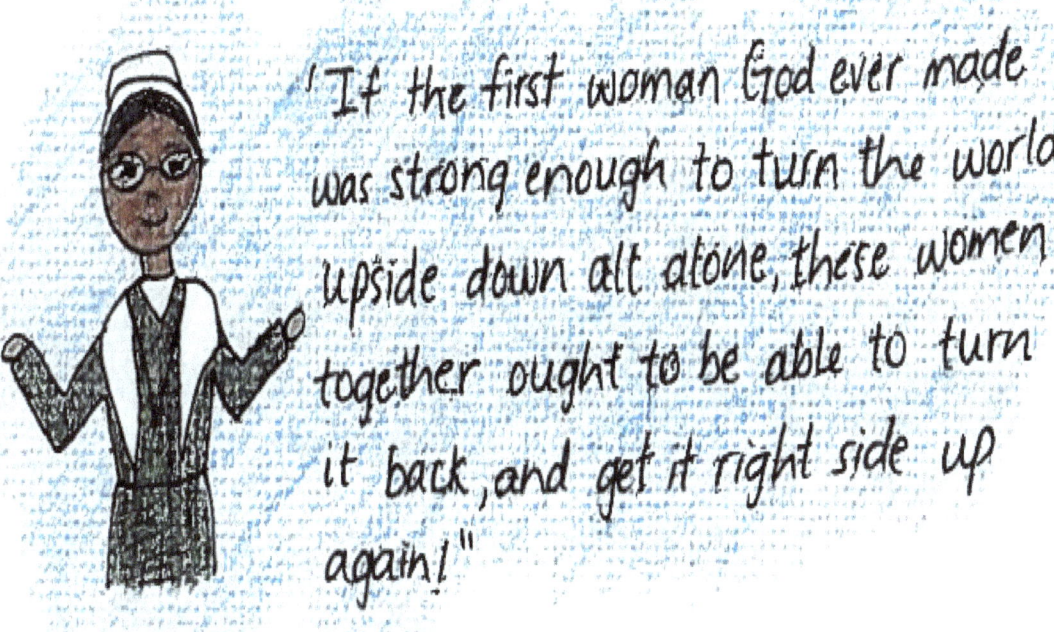

"If the first woman God ever made was strong enough to turn the world upside down all alone, these women together ought to be able to turn it back, and get it right side up again!"

Ss

S is for Sappho, an ancient artful poet. She found love and beauty with other women and used her poems to show it.

"O Venus, beauty of the skies,
To whom a thousand temples rise,
Gaily false in gentle smiles,
Full of love-perplexing wiles,"

Tt

T is for thoughtful, like Mother Teresa and Dorothy Day.
Just because the world has poverty doesn't mean it has to stay.

what we have we share

we don't need material things

economic justice is a must

everybody deserves to be loved

feed those who are hungry

live with people in poverty

Uu

U is for unbroken, despite some trying times. Hardship tried to bring Maya Angelou down but she rose up with her rhymes

"you may shoot me down with your words,
you may cut me with your eyes,
you may kill me with your hatefulness,
but still, like air, I'll rise"

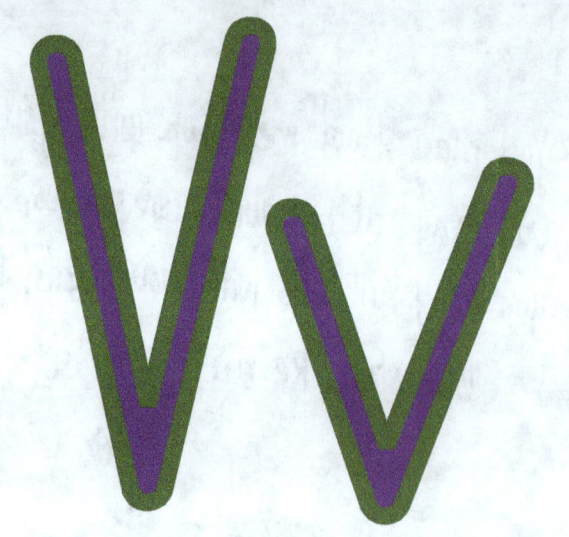

V is for Virginia Woolf, a smart and daring writer. She wrote her books when men said no and for that she was a fighter.

W is for warrior, though a peaceful loving kind. They waged a war against oppression keeping freedom on their minds.

Xx

X is for compassion, which doesn't start with X. We can bend the rules to show compassion 'cause that's what revolutionaries do best.

"I will not pay taxes to fund the war!"

Dorothy Day

"I will not pray to a male God that says women are a problem"

Mary Daly

Yy

Y is for you, because you are wonderful too! You can find your strength in all these women who are here to see you through.

Zz

Z is for zealous, a passion without end. Fight for justice with all your might and always be a friend.

About Nora

Nora Kane is currently a senior at Wake Forest University and will be graduating in May 2015. She is majoring in Religious Studies with a concentration in Religion and Public Engagement and minoring in French. This book was created as a midterm project for Dr. Angela Yarber's Women's and Gender Studies class "Women, History, and Myth".

www.ingramcontent.com/pod-product-compliance
Lightning Source LLC
Chambersburg PA
CBHW081403290426
44110CB00018B/2473